Ann Elizabeth Signs with Love

Jesus loves me

written by
Annetta E. Dellinger

Micha

CONCORDIA

2094

Thanks to Ann Elizabeth Boerger.

Special thanks to Rev. Don Leber, Holy Cross Lutheran Church for the Deaf, Columbus, Ohio, for his help with this book. He along with Rev. Gary Lawson and Rev. Shirrel Petzoldt—three very enthusiastic and dedicated pastors who work in deaf ministry—have touched many people with Jesus' love.

The setting for "Jesus Loves Me, This I Know" is from *A Child's Garden of Song* © 1949 by Concordia Publishing House.

Copyright © 1991 Concordia Publishing House
3558 S. Jefferson Avenue, St. Louis, MO 63118-3968
Manufactured in the United States of America

Library of Congress Cataloging-in-Publication Data
Dellinger, Annetta E.
    Ann Elizabeth signs with love/Annetta E. Dellinger
    Summary: A deaf child demonstrates in sign language the words to the song "Jesus Loves Me" and also tells of her love for her family.
    ISBN 0-570-04192-9
    1. Children, Deaf—Religious life—Juvenile literature. 2. Sign language—Juvenile literature. [1. Christian life. 2. Sign language.] I. Title.
HV2392.D45   1991
248.8'2—dc20   90-38171
                                                                        CIP
                                                                        AC

1 2 3 4 5 6 7 8 9 10   00 99 98 97 96 95 94 93 92 91

Dear Parents,

It is easy and fun to teach young children sign language. Learning sign language will help them understand how God helps people who are deaf communicate.

It is my prayer that through this book you and your child will be able to tell a person who is deaf about Jesus. What joy will fill your hearts as you share His love.

Joyfully,

Annetta E. Dellinger

Hi, I am Ann Elizabeth. I can stand on my head and turn cartwheels. I can almost read, and I can count to 100. I live with my family in a big, yellow house.

My mommy has blond, curly hair. She almost always has a big smile on her face. She wears glasses to help her see better.

My daddy is tall. He has a brown mustache that curls up on the ends. My brother John is smaller than I am. John and I have a little, fluffy puppy named Peanut Butter.

Grandpa lives with our family, too. He and I like to go for walks. I hold his hand because I love him. He uses a cane to help him walk better.

My family has fun together. We play games. Sometimes I win. We go fishing down by the pond and then have a picnic. John and I even help Mommy bake chocolate chip cookies. Yum!

I know my family loves me. They give me hugs and kisses. They tell me they love me with their hands because I cannot hear them. I am deaf.

I love my family, too. I tell them by the special way I move my hands. It's called sign language. This means "I love you." Can you say, *I love you*, with your hands?

Hold right palm facing outward. Extend thumb, index finger, and pinky finger. Keep middle and ring fingers folded down.

9

There is someone else who loves my family very much. He loves me too! We are each special to Him. It is Jesus. I love Him very much.

I like to sing "Jesus Loves Me" with my hands. Will you help me?

Jesus

1. Hold open palms facing each other.

2. Touch the left palm with the right middle finger.

3. Touch the right palm with the left middle finger.

loves

Cross fists over heart.

me,

Point index finger toward chest.

11

this

1. Hold left hand with palm facing upward.

2. Touch the center of the left palm with the right index finger

I

1. Place right hand on chest, palm facing left and thumb touching chest.

2. Hold pinky finger straight up. Fold index, middle, and ring finger down.

12

know,

1. Slightly curve fingers on right hand.
2. Tap fingers on forehead several times.

For

1. Touch right side of forehead with index finger.

2. Immediately dip index finger until it is pointing straight ahead.

(The word *the* is not signed.)

Bible

The word *Jesus* is signed first with a second sign for *book* added.

1. Hold open palms facing each other.

2. Touch the left palm with right middle finger.

3. Touch the right palm with left middle finger.

4. Put hands together with palms touching.

5. Open palms as if opening a book.

15

tells me

1. Make small forward circular movements in front of mouth with right index finger.

2. Move right index finger to point to center of chest.

so.

1. Hold left palm face up.

2. Place right fist with thumb and p extended into left palm.

(The word *that* is signed for the word s

Little ones

1. With right palm facing downward pretend to pat the tops of several children's heads from left to right.

(The word *children* is signed for *little ones*.)

Him

(The word *to* is not signed.)

1. Hold open palms facing each other about 6 inches apart.

2. Touch left palm with right middle finger.

3. Touch right palm with left middle finger.

(The word *Jesus* is signed for *Him.*)

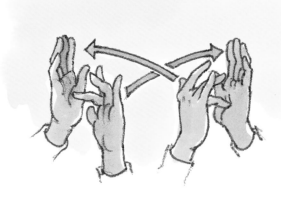

18

belong.

1. Interlock index fingers and thumbs of both hands.
2. Extend other fingers.

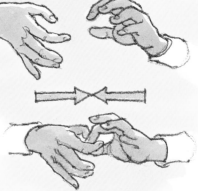

They   are

1. Point right index finger and move from left to right.

1. Move right index finger in a forward arch from lips, palm facing left.

(The word *you* is signed for *they*.)

weak,

1. Hold left palm flat, facing upward.

2. Curve fingers of right hand in a standing position on left palm.

3. Bend and unbend fingers.

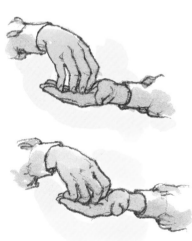

but

1. With palms facing out, cross tips of both index fingers.

2. Move index fingers a short distance apart.

21

He

1. Hold open palms facing each other about six inches apart.

2. Touch left palm with the right middle finger.

3. Touch the right palm with the left middle finger.

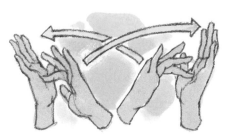

(The word *Jesus* is signed for *He*.)

is

1. Move right index finger in a forward arch from lips, palm facing left.

strong.

1. Make a fist with both hands, palms facing each other.

2. Move fists downward with a strong motion.

Yes,   Jesus

Make fist with right hand, shake up and down as if nodding.

1. Hold open palms facing each other.

2. Touch left palm with the right middle finger.

3. Touch right palm with the left middle finger.

ves

me,

s fists over

Point right index finger toward chest.

(Repeat *Yes, Jesus loves me* three times. The word *the* is not signed.)

Bible

1. Hold open palms facing each other.
2. Touch left palm with right middle finger.
3. Touch right palm with left middle finger.
4. Put hands together with palms touching.
5. Open palms as if opening a book.

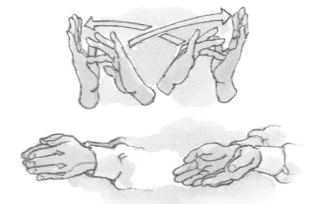

tells me

1. Make small forward circular movements in front of mouth with right index finger.

2. Move right index finger to point to center of chest.

so.

1. Hold left palm face up.

2. Place right fist with thumb and pinky extended into left palm.

Jesus loves me.

Jesus loves you too!

Jesus loves me

Anna B. Warner, 1820–1915

William B. Bradbury, 1816–68

Je - sus loves me, this I know, For the Bi - ble tells me so.

Lit - tle ones to Him be - long; They are weak, but He is strong.

Refrain

Yes, Je - sus loves me, Yes, Je - sus loves me.

Yes, Je - sus loves me, The Bi - ble tells me so.